Listening to Kathy

JO SCOTT-COE

BIG JACARANDA BOOKS
Riverside, California

Listening to Kathy
Copyright © 2016 by Scott-Coe, Jo
ISBN: 9780692747971
All rights reserved

Adapted from "Listening to Kathy" as published on Catapult.co, March 30, 2016

No part of this book may be used or reproduced in any manner whatsoever without the prior written permission of the copyright owner.

Cover Image: Kathy Leissner in 1962, before her marriage to Charles Whitman.

Book design and layout by Dean Vergara
All photographs courtesy of Nelson Leissner

Printed and bound in the United States
Distributed by Ingram

Published by Big Jacaranda Books
Riverside, CA
Second Edition

In memory of
KATHLEEN, MARGARET, AND FRANCES

Preface

In a digital age, a story can find an audience across the world in a relatively short period of time. Despite the advantages of omnipresent access, readers can still miss the tactility of the three-dimensional experience, a longing that may apply most when a story is elegiac in nature and when body memory is precisely what seems misplaced.

This reprint of "Listening to Kathy" seeks to put the story of Kathy Leissner Whitman into the hands of those for whom a material remembrance is important. In addition to the photographs originally published when this article appeared in *Catapult* earlier this year, readers will now find more images in a supplemental photo album.

Kathy's letters to her family, and especially to her mother, Frances, are the closest thing to a personal diary that has survived, revealing day-to-day reflections of a young woman sorting out challenges of freedom and confinement at the beginning of a marriage, and during a time of mixed messages and opportunities. The extraordinary correspondence provides a glimpse of the relationship between two women who sought to maintain their bond during geographical and circumstantial separation. For this reason, the letters must be respected as primary documentation within women's history rather than as a mere footnote in one man's "true crime" narrative.

Kathy's mother—college educated and teaching by the time of her marriage in 1939—is a remarkable presence, her voice insightful, by turns diplomatic and direct. One can feel her navigating a difficult maternal struggle: the instinct to protect one's child versus the desire to preserve all possible lines of communication with an independent adult.

The progression of Kathy's letters dramatizes her development as a thinker and as her own best advocate. It is a cruel irony that the newlywed separation causing her so much worry and pain also gave her space to discover herself and develop her own talents. Sadly, her much-anticipated reunion with her husband was more romantic on paper and from a distance than in real life. Like so many women, including her mother-in-law Margaret, Kathy did not have enough time to make her best intentions take full flight. Her life and her hopes for change were brutally stolen from her.

Kathy lived at an important historical moment, as women's college enrollment began its unstoppable surge. The National Center for Education Statistics (NCES) documents that in 1961, Kathy's first semester at University of Texas at Austin, the total percentage of U.S. female high school graduates enrolling in college was 41.3%, up from 37.9% in 1960—an increase of 52 thousand female students nationally in just one year. By 1965, the year Kathy accepted her college diploma, the total percentage of women's enrollment had risen to 45.3%, an increase of 234 thousand students within four years.

Women were not universally welcomed on campus at the time. In one letter, Kathy described how a professor insisted on separating women from men in his classroom. The social latitude afforded to the Mad Men of the same generation was extreme, while young women could still, under the law, be openly discriminated against or harassed in the workplace. "Girls" were still largely expected to exhibit charm above all else, a phenomenon Kathy alluded to in describing her exhausting night in the coat-check for a friend's reception: "I'm so tired of smiling at rich old men!"

Importantly, Kathy was wedded in 1962 at age nineteen, before contraception was a legal right for individuals or even married couples, and when the subjects of child abuse and domestic violence remained largely taboo. Separation and divorce were still rare. LGBTQ citizens risked social ostracism or worse unless they lived closeted lives or opted for "treatment." The closest thing to any intellectual discussion of gender roles or sexuality in college was a 1964 "Marriage and Family Life" course that Kathy described in letters to her husband, a course that she said she "loved" and wanted her husband to take.

Given her uniquely stressful domestic circumstances, the achievement of a college degree testifies to Kathy's fortitude and determination, as well as the inspiration and support of her parents. There are hints that Kathy's celebration of this milestone may have been muted, no doubt in part because her husband was so far from meeting any goals of his own. The only surviving photograph I found documenting

Kathy's graduation day is a badly lit snapshot from Jack's Party Pictures showing her in cap and gown, shaking hands with a college official on the dais.

There are reasons to say that times have changed, that we celebrate diversity, equality, and women's achievements more than ever now in the United States. Congress passed the Civil Rights Act in 1964, the Equal Employment Opportunity Act and Title IX in 1972. Court rulings have advanced women's reproductive freedom (though not without controversy and pushback), and divorce has lost its stigma. LGBTQ Americans have made significant strides, and same-sex couples now have the right to marry no matter what state they live in.

Despite fifty years of progress, challenges remain. By 1980, the enrollment of women in college actually eclipsed that of men, yet according to the most recent Census in 2014, more than one in seven adult women live in poverty. By 2015, women still represented only 19.4% of US Congress members and, in 2016, only 4.6% of CEO positions at S&P 500 companies. Gender hostility remains more than an abstraction. In 2011, the Center for Disease Control reported that 35.6% of women—more than one third—experienced rape, physical violence, or stalking by an intimate partner in their lifetime. That's approximately 42.4 million women.

These lingering realities may explain why Kathy's story, and others like hers, might be difficult to see or to hear.

Indeed, it took a while to find a magazine willing to publish this essay. Audiences of mass media tend to reserve their outrage for particular types of violence, often withholding empathy when it comes to domestic abuse. Perhaps writers and editors sense this on a primal level. To some extent, collectively, whether we admit it or not, we still blame the victim at home. "Why did she stay?" we ask, rather than, "How could he do that?" or "What can we do together to disrupt the pattern?"

As we prepared this reprint, the shooting rampage at Pulse nightclub in Orlando—now the most deadly attack of its kind on American soil—demonstrated yet again how intersections of fear and hate have deadly consequences. The shooter had a record of domestic abuse in his first marriage, and his attack targeted a "safe zone" for both LGBTQ and Hispanic-Latino communities in Florida.

I hope I will live to see the transformation of this conversation, so that those who find themselves living with domestic abuse can get resources and support without judgment, stigma, and dismissal. We have a long way to go before we stop enabling the real threat of homegrown terror next door.

I am grateful to Kathy's brother, Nelson, who trusted me with details and artifacts of his sister's life. I am also indebted to her other brothers, Ray and Adam, along with family members, and friends, who took the time to communicate their memories.

Finally, I want to thank my original editors at *Catapult*, Mensah Demary and Yuka Igarashi, who understood from the onset that Kathy's story had been missing from the record for far too long.

Jo Scott-Coe
July 1, 2016
Riverside CA

· Listening to Kathy ·

It was humid the morning of August 3, 1966, in the quiet farm community of Needville, Texas, where one family lingered alone at the funeral home for a last look at the face of their only daughter and sister, Kathleen ("Kathy") Leissner. Two days earlier, she had been brutally stabbed in her own bed by her husband, Charles Whitman, during the dark hours before he climbed the University of Texas at Austin's landmark tower and became the Texas Sniper. Kathy had just turned twenty-three.

Her life and its violent ending were smothered by the spectacle of her husband's 96-minute rampage—at the time, the most fatal mass shooting in US history. As he terrorized downtown Austin, Whitman killed or wounded more than forty people, including students, local residents, and campus visitors. He struck a permanent blow, on national television, to the belief that some public spaces were sanctuaries rather than war zones.

But Whitman's coldly calculated shots from the tower had been preceded by two personal murders the night before: his mother, Margaret, and then his wife, Kathy. For those two women and their families, domestic terror had a private face.

The collision of a public crisis with a violation so intimate, permanent, and unthinkable—committed by a man they thought they knew—added an extra layer of devastation for Kathy's family. At home, 150 miles south of Austin, they shuttered their pain outside the public eye.

Kathy's three brothers—Nelson (then nineteen), Ray, Jr. (then fourteen) and Adam (only twenty-one months)—had no vocabulary for their shock.

Nelson recalled, "I remember going to a local gas station and filling up one of the trucks. It was total silence. Heads down. I thought, maybe it's out of respect for us. They didn't know what to say, and I certainly didn't know what to say back."

"People did not want to stir those feelings," said a cousin, Nancy Bartosh, who had been Kathy's maid of honor.

The speechlessness was a painful paradox in the heart of a tragedy that led to such national frenzy. Kathy's mother and father never made more than a few comments in public.

As years passed, Nelson quietly safeguarded photo albums and his sister's belongings, including a childhood scrapbook now held together with blue rubber bands. From a family member's driveway, he rescued a cardboard box containing her handwritten letters, mistakenly left out with the garbage.

"So many things I don't remember because of the horror of losing her," Nelson said. "I just went blank. That I regret.

Nelson (left) presents his sister with a rose the night she represented Needville in the Fort Bend County Fair.

But I know in my heart that somebody needs to remember her. And I thought, that's got to be me."

For a long time I had been writing about violence in public spaces, especially schools. I paid particular attention to the strange silence around the experiences of those—often women—who knew the perpetrators beforehand and had been preliminary witnesses to, or targets of, escalating aggression and abuse.

In 2014, while completing a book on the religious and cultural context of the UT shooting, I wrote to Nelson seeking information about his sister's marriage ceremony. We met for the first time in Texas almost a year later. Nelson showed me Kathy's *peau de soie* wedding dress, stored tenderly in its original garment bag. Laid across the bed, the empty gown looked delicate and impossibly small.

As the fiftieth anniversary of her death neared, Nelson consulted Ray and Adam. "I want to do something for Kathy," he said. "Mother and Dad have passed away—nothing can hurt them anymore." Understandably wary about media, the brothers eventually agreed.

In the five decades since that horrible day for so many people, the story had never before been approached from Kathy's perspective or included her words.

With the help of her family and friends, Kathy's life could finally, and for the very first time, become part of the record.

Nelson sent me a list of contacts. We talked for hours on the phone. And then two large packages arrived on my doorstep. I opened them up.

*I*n diaries and letters preserved by the FBI investigation, Charles Whitman often referred to Kathy as his "most precious possession."

But to her family, she was neither a possession nor a victim. As her mother, Frances, wrote in a letter to her son-in-law: "Kathy, until her marriage, has always been a normal, healthy, well-adjusted person with many friends and secure in the knowledge that she was loved and needed, a person, not a doormat."

Frances was a college graduate when she married Raymond Leissner in 1939. She began teaching English at age eighteen. Raymond inherited acreage in Needville, where he worked tirelessly year-round as both cattle rancher and rice farmer. He would later own a real estate business.

Kathy was their first child and only daughter, born July 12, 1943, at Dow Magnesium Hospital. In one of her baby books, next to "date for first crawl" a note from Frances said: "Walked first."

Growing up, Kathy was more than Needville Youth Fair Queen and candidate for Fort Bend County Fair Queen. She contributed to nearly every possible aspect of school and small-town life. She sang alto in the Methodist Church choir and went on hayrides with the youth group. She played tenor sax in the school band, acted in the senior play, wrote columns for The Blue Jay Chatter, played volleyball, was head twirler, served as art editor for the annual, and was vice president of Future Homemakers of America, She also learned about work, driving the rice truck on her father's farm, and with Nelson, helping to herd cattle.

Between the ages of ten and fifteen, Kathy kept a large scrapbook of ordinary joys in her life. She pasted streamers and invitations from birthday parties, soda straws and spoons, purple and white taffeta "spirit ribbons" for football and basketball games. She kept letters from her mother on a trip and letters she decided not to send to boys.

There are poignant signals of the transition to womanhood. Corsages pressed in their original cellophane. An unsent postcard with three bright blots of pink lipstick on the back. A Modess calendar from 1956-57, torn into four pieces and stashed into a paper pocket among birthday cards. A playbill for Frank Sinatra in *Joker is Wild* from a "first date," along with a pressed box of Welch's Pom Poms.

Near the end is one page she labeled "The Most Wonderful Night of the Year." Here, Kathy taped a packet of wax paper containing mud from her shoes. "We played Eagle Lake," she wrote. "I walked Milton off the field . . . So-o-o-o-o HAPPY."

Kathy, as hostess, serving cake at a party for a Needville High School club.

*Kathy dancing with her high school sweetheart.
The couple's matching dress and shirt were made by her mother.*

Most yearbook images capture Kathy's bright and twinkling presence among her classmates. But in a picture for the National Honors Society, Kathy sits back, unsmiling, in the shadows on the steps. For one moment, she retreated into her thoughts, not performing for anyone.

Kathy graduated in May 1961 and planned to attend UT Austin to study pharmacy, a fact confirmed by her first semester transcript. Hurricane Carla stormed the region for two weeks that September, and during the chaos and recovery, the family trusted Kathy's longtime sweetheart, Lawrence, to drive Kathy to register for classes.

In the senior newspaper, among classmates' farewell messages, Kathy had effused, "I had a grand time and I'll miss it terribly." As she moved to a big college city, she must have anticipated new freedom and independence.

"She could've married the president," said Marje Janacek, one of Kathy's best friends from childhood through high school. "She would have made a wonderful first lady."

Before her sophomore year of college, she married someone else.

Kathy Leissner and Charles J. Whitman as a new couple in February 1962.

*C*harlie Whitman's introduction to Kathy's family was sudden. The couple met in February 1962, and she brought him home that spring. It was immediately serious. No one knew Charlie's family, and he had no ties to Needville.

"I'll never forget as long as I live," Nelson said. "It was 'Hey, Nelson! How are you?' Big ol' handshake. Big Ipana smile. Blond, clean-cut. When he walked through the door and into the den, he said, 'Wow. This is a huge house. How much did this cost?'"

Nelson was amazed by the calm response of his father, who offered one polite, cautioning rejoinder to Charlie's impolite question: "It cost enough." Raymond always demanded respect, and he had once gently chided Lawrence—whom the family loved—for honking his horn in the driveway when running late with Kathy to meet friends.

"Charlie did such a snow job," Nelson said. "He was going to be an engineer and he worshipped the ground Kathy walked on, and blah blah blah. Normally Daddy didn't fall for that."

What happened when Kathy asked what Nelson thought? "I told her: 'He's not Lawrence.' She wasn't mad, but she said, 'I know, but he's really special to me.'"

In July, newspapers announced Kathy's engagement. A rush of preparations followed: bridal showers, dress fittings, and a luncheon and fashion show at Houston's Normandie Restaurant. A photo from one party shows Kathy cutting the sheet cake, a flashbulb bursting white light in the mirror behind her.

The Leissners met Charlie's mother, father, and two brothers for the first time just before the wedding, which was held at St. Michael's parish in Needville. The pretty church, which could have been carved from blocks of white sugar, remains virtually unchanged. The ceremony date was August 17—the wedding anniversary of Charlie's parents.

While the newlyweds honeymooned in New Orleans, Nelson was invited to vacation with the Whitmans at their home in Florida. He witnessed firsthand the family his sister had married into. Charlie's father screamed at his wife and sons, and even flung a pan across the kitchen during a dinner tirade. Nelson also didn't like how the man talked to him. "He said he thought he could knock some sense into me. I wanted out of there."

By the time Kathy and Charlie arrived, it was difficult for Nelson to talk with his sister privately. When he eventually did—in the aisle of a grocery market—he explained that he wanted to leave discreetly to help their father with the rice harvest. But Kathy told her husband, who told his father. "It was a big blowup," Nelson said. "I think Charlie realized then that I didn't trust him. But they were married. Back then, they're *married*."

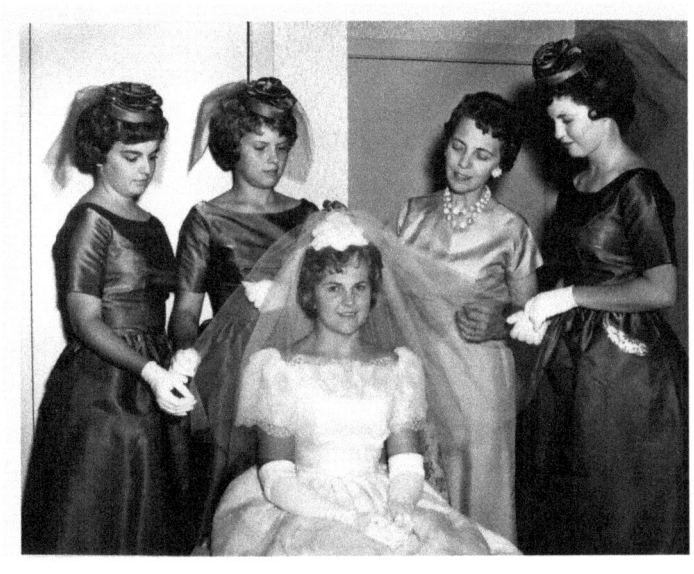

Wedding Day: 17 August 1962. Kathy attended by her mother, Frances, and bridesmaids.

As the honeymoon ended and Kathy and Charlie began their adjustment to life as married college students, they faced an additional challenge. During the holidays, Charlie's parents sent one of his troubled brothers to live with the newlyweds in their small apartment.

The extra responsibility only contributed more stress. A letter to Charlie from Frances, just five months after the wedding, revealed that she was attuned to her daughter's unhappiness. Citing Charlie's statement that Kathy had changed, Frances agreed: "She is about the most miserable young woman—and she is a young woman, not a child, as you seem to think, who is trying to make a marriage work." But to Charlie's suggestion that Kathy needed a psychiatrist, Frances disagreed unequivocally: "I am a woman, just as Kathy is, and I know you feel that no woman can think logically. But I shall try... By trying to completely dominate Kathy you are destroying the very things which attracted you to her in the first place." She urged the couple to visit a marriage counselor. "You both know you are not happy with this marriage," she wrote. "Then do the logical thing and go to someone who can help both of you."

In early February, Kathy wrote to tell her mother her brother-in-law had left and that she and Charlie were "getting along 100% better," although she admitted to a lingering "horror" that he would lose his military scholarship due to unsatisfactory academic performance. It didn't help, she said, that her in-laws created tension when they called: "[Charlie] always seems to get the same lecture about what a disgraceful son he is."

Kathy's fears were prescient. Within only a few days, Charlie lost his scholarship and withdrew from classes, returning to Marine Corps active duty at Camp Lejeune in North Carolina. Kathy withdrew from school immediately to join him. In a letter postmarked on Valentine's Day, she shared the bad news with her mother: "The only thing that will be hard on me is to leave you, & Daddy, & Nelson, & Ray for so long… I sure do hate to leave Texas. I guess maybe I'm not grown up yet even if I am 19 years old."

Kathy assured her mother that she would finish her education somehow, and made a plea on her husband's behalf: "After Charlie talked to Daddy last night he said he thought you both regretted my marrying him . . . I hope you will make him feel that he's not considered the biggest louse in the world." She added, "Tell everyone hello for us and explain what happened."

Three days a week from mid-March through early July 1963, Charlie was away on base maneuvers, training for the machine gun squad, and Kathy was left to fend for herself in their Jacksonville apartment: "It sure is terrible to be so alone," she wrote. "Mother, did you know that the life expectancy of a machine gunner is exactly 6 sec. after the 1st shot of battle?"

In several hundred pages of letters during this period, Kathy's voice has been preserved, revealing her isolation as well as her brave face. The correspondence was a crucial lifeline during a time when she did not have a phone. "You don't know how much better they make me feel," Kathy wrote, referring to her mother's letters and pictures that spring. "I've worn them out already."

Kathy composed most of her thoughts while biding time—waiting for Charlie to return, for the carburetor to be adjusted, for her job applications to be reviewed. She spit-shined her husband's boots. She rose at 5:00 AM to make his breakfast before he departed on Tuesday mornings. She seemed to do an endless amount of laundry: "I'm writing you on the back of a box of Cheer," she wrote. "I'm writing from the washateria (as usual)."

Kathy's pages provide an intimate snapshot of her life, and the lives of many military wives. She babysat for neighbors, changed her hair color ("Champagne toast, Lady Clairol"), worried about whether new recipes for lasagna and angel cake would please her husband. Movies provided a modicum of pleasure with Charlie on weekends (she recommended *Giant* and *To Kill a Mockingbird*). Money was tight. In the search for a job, she described one interview where she was turned down because she was married: "I did everything but tell them I was taking Enovid!" she wrote. When she finally secured a job at a pawnshop, the hours were extreme: from noon to 10 PM. Even then, her wages were not her own: "Charlie said I could have 20% of my salary to spend on anything I want," she told her mother. Her plan was to scrape dollars together for extension classes.

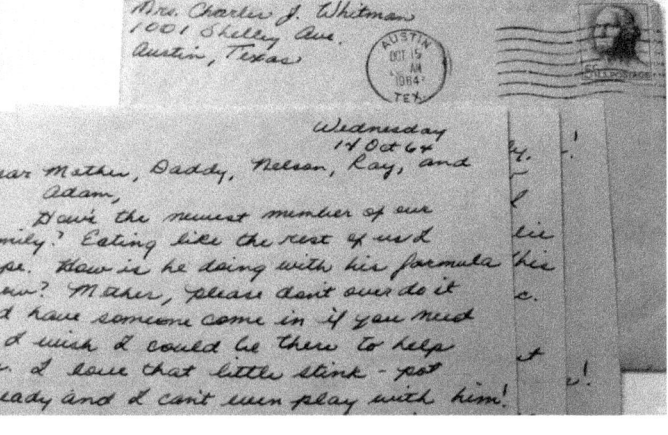

One of Kathy's letters to her family, dated Wednesday, October 14, 1964, shortly following Adam's birth.

During this time, Kathy repeated often how she felt surrounded by pregnant women: "I really am out of style," she joked. But while she longed for a child, she also expressed relief when she did not conceive. Many women around her were parenting without spouses. One neighbor who gave birth to a stillborn suffered a hemorrhage two weeks later. Kathy and another woman drove her to the hospital and arranged her childcare the following day.

Kathy put off telling her family about a car accident that had taken place weeks before, on the route to Jacksonville. "We didn't tell anyone because you were doing enough worrying about us," she wrote. "Needless to say, it put us in a tight bind for funds. In fact, we are still feeling it." She also understated Charlie's odd behavior, such as one night when he told her to change clothes, then moved all furniture from the kitchen to the living room so he could fit a mattress on the floor: "Then he proceeded to show me all the new judo holds he had learned that day. I don't know why he thinks I have to know judo! I was so worn out I was in bed at 9:00."

Frances's letters to Kathy communicate steadiness, realism, and urgency, too: "If you have to be a fighting Marine," she said, addressing Charlie, "I'm sure you'll be a credit to the Corps. I can't think of a thing to say that doesn't sound trite and stupid. You know damn well that we are thinking of you all constantly, and pray you come back to us when this hitch is over." She sent books, candy, copies of the *Gulf Coast Tribune*, an Easter basket. She told Kathy that she shared her letters but would stop if Kathy preferred: "Everybody wants to know how you are. You know, you have a lot of friends."

When it emerged that Charlie would likely be sent to Cuba or to Haiti, Frances encouraged her daughter to come home on the family's dime. At first Kathy was not sure. "He has some phobia about me going home, so to save the marriage I guess I'll stay," she wrote. Eventually, however, she would wriggle free.

Days before her return, Charlie made a secret appeal to his mother-in-law, adding onto one of Kathy's letters after she departed for work: "I sure wish you could talk my wife into having a baby," he wrote. He included a film recommendation of his own: *The Ugly American*.

That summer, Nelson helped Kathy pack up and return to Texas. After less than one year of marriage, from July 1963 to December 1964—a year and a half—Kathy lived apart from her husband. She functioned quite well when she was no longer directly under his thumb. Living with friends near UT, she enrolled in a teacher education program, worked to pay bills, studied, performed well on exams, and visited her family.

But it was not easy living as a newlywed without a spouse. Communication from her husband was spotty during this period, in part because Charlie spent weeks on duty at GITMO. Early on, apparently following an argument by phone, Kathy stated that she was going to stop worrying about her husband's card games: "I've decided to stop being the nagging wife," she said. She spent her first wedding anniversary alone and did not hear from Charlie until days afterwards. But she felt bad for another reason: "I want to apologize for complaining about not hearing from you," she wrote, following receipt of two letters. "I hope you will forgive me. You sounded mad in your letter and I just cried. Please, don't be mad at me."

Rather than heeding his wife's good judgment, Charlie landed in serious trouble not only for gambling, but also for lending money "at usurious rates" and possessing an unauthorized firearm. Even in the brig, he took little responsibility: "The Govt just doesn't go along with my loan business," he wrote to Kathy's parents. Pictures show that Kathy traveled to stand with him the day of his court martial. He was sentenced to hard labor and demoted to Private.

By spring 1964, as her second semester of classes drew to a close, Kathy's reflections about her relationship deepened, becoming more gently assertive. "I feel like our marriage has been strengthened, but only because of the many trials we've been through, not because we've been together and talked about our ideas and plans," she wrote to Charlie. "We have both changed a lot I'm sure, and we are both going to have to realize that when we get back together and respect each other's new ideas."

For their second anniversary, Charlie sent Kathy a card that included a strange declaration of his love: "My Darling if there were any way that I could give you the greatest thing

I possess—you, my wife—I would fully give yourself to you. Sounds foolish, doesn't it? . . . Maybe some day the intensity of my love for you will strike you."

Once discharged in December 1964, he reunited with Kathy in Austin to catch up on his own studies and cobble jobs together. Kathy completed student teaching, graduated, and crossed her fingers for a full-time position, which she secured easily. A letter to her family in May 1965 hinted at continued loneliness despite the couple's reunion: "I feel these days like I am keeping house for a ghost."

Kathy became a biology teacher in fall 1965 at Sidney Lanier High School. By February 1966, she wrote to her parents from an afternoon study hall, expressing cheerful self-deprecation about the stellar review she received from the principal in a conference earlier that day: "He rated me 'strong' on practically everything. How he justifies his evaluation, I'll never know, as he's never even been in my classroom!"

Kathy looked forward to accepting an assignment the following year at a brand new high school. She also welcomed her mother-in-law, Margaret, who in March moved to Austin seeking a divorce from her husband of twenty-five years. But there would be no new start for Margaret, and Kathy's first year teaching would be her last.

Kathy (center) with her mother-in-law, Margaret (left), and her mother, Frances (right).

*F*BI records reveal that Charlie likely abused Kathy—at least twice, according to admissions he made to a psychiatrist about "assaulting" her. But though she openly feared his temper, Kathy never reported physical violence to anyone, and no one in her family had witnessed it. "If we had known," said Nelson, "I think Daddy would have killed Charlie himself."

In spring 1966, Kathy traveled alone to Needville to visit her parents. Nelson overheard them. "I wasn't supposed to know anything," he said. "Kathy had some pride. We knew Charlie wasn't looking so polished anymore. But I'll never forget. Kathy says, 'You know, Dad, I love Charlie. But I wish to God I'd never met him.'"

His father asked whether Charlie had hurt her, and Kathy's denial was mixed: "No," she said, "but he can be violent."

"Then get rid of him," Nelson heard his father say. "Before he kills you."

Nelson recalled Kathy recoiling. "I remember her reacting like, 'Oh Daddy. Good God. Why would you say something like that?'"

Early that summer, in mid-July, Ray visited Austin and stayed with his sister and her husband for about two weeks. "I sat in on some classes at UT with Charlie that week," Ray said. "I had absolutely no clue that anything was amiss." He added, "But I was a teenager."

The last weekend Kathy was alive, Nelson brought Adam up from Needville to visit, and they, too, returned home without incident.

Late on the night before the shootings, Marje called Kathy to coordinate outfits for their upcoming class reunion. "I called two or three times and no answer," she said. "Her mother later told me they found Kathy's tissue paper pattern and fabric laid out, pinned and everything, for the dress she had been making. Right there on the kitchen table."

Around noon on August 1, Nelson was washing his mother's car. His portable radio erupted with news about a shooter on the tower at UT Austin, but Nelson did not think of Kathy. He knew she was working at the phone company during the summer, and he figured Charlie was safe inside a classroom.

When his brother, Ray, and a friend announced they wanted to go swimming, Nelson offered to take them in the truck. He dropped them off and went to check the levies in the rice fields, then joined them for a dip. The artesian tanks always provided welcome relief in the beastly summer.

The boys noticed unusual activity when they returned to town. "A ton of cars and people around dad's little real estate office," Nelson said.

Approaching the house, they saw even more cars and trucks alongside the road, TV cameras and policemen everywhere.

When Nelson parked and walked towards the house, he saw the justice of the peace. "I asked what was going on, and the justice broke down and cried. He said, 'Leave him alone. Let him get through.' I pushed somehow through the garage and into the kitchen. There were people everywhere. I was trying to get to dad, and I couldn't find him. I went into the den and couldn't find him.

"The TV was on. It was about the sniper and the shooting. Someone said, 'Nelson, Charlie has killed people.' And that's when it hit me. On the TV screen, there was my sister's body being brought out of the house."

Nelson's father disappeared. His mother drove the car out to the ranch. "She ran into the barn," said Nelson. "Dad was just sitting there, in total darkness. And he was crying. Mother told me later that she had been afraid he was going to kill himself."

Kathy's white casket, almost entirely covered by a mound of pink carnations, was carried from the Methodist Church by young men who had grown up with her. Ray, Jr. recalled, "I remember the huge line of cars—I had never seen anything like that before." Mourners spilled outside and stood wherever they could.

Many young people had anticipated greeting Kathy only a few days later at their fifth year reunion. Instead, they said goodbye at Davis-Greenlawn Cemetery in nearby

Rosenberg. Woody Bacica, a classmate and pallbearer, said, "Kathy coming back to Needville that way—it was a terrible event."

The 1966 class reunion was held in her honor, and to the present day her memory is included in the gatherings. Marje said, "When she died, we were all just eternally bonded."

For the family, Kathy's memory was not allowed to rest in peace after the burial. Nelson recalled news vans lingering, the FBI showing up with questions. Hundreds of condolence cards and letters crowded the family post office box, with many messages lashing out in blame rather than sympathy.

It was too much to absorb. As the intrusions ceased and public attention faded, Kathy's parents and brothers were left to deal with the grief in their own individual ways. "We were in such shock," Nelson said. "We kind of lived in our own shells. We really did."

After Kathy's death, everything changed. Nelson, Ray, Jr., and Adam grew up, entered adulthood, and carried on without their eldest sibling.

Ray remembered her beauty. He also said, "She would take my side when Nelson and I got into an argument—I appreciated that."

As an infant, Adam had been doted upon by Kathy, but he only came to know her through photographs. Her room remained pretty much as she had left it. His parents even kept a picture of Charlie on the wall. "They were remarkable," Adam said. "They were able to forgive him."

Nelson entered the Air Force in 1969. When his service concluded and he returned home in 1973, his parents divorced. After thirty-two years of marriage, his father had confessed to having an affair for more than a decade. Both parents went on to long second marriages.

Adam's birth, Nelson believes, ultimately saved his mother's life. The day her only daughter was murdered, when neighbors burst into the house, Frances had been napping with her little boy. "She told me later," Nelson said. "She realized that she could go insane, but she chose to take care of her son."

Adam's memory confirmed this. "My mother never let me see what she must have been feeling," he said.

All three brothers left Needville eventually. All three maintained connections to their parents. Frances passed away in 2008. Raymond died in 2010.

*N*elson's favorite picture of Kathy, an informal portrait now kept in a frame at Adam's house, was taken some time before her marriage, when she was eighteen.

Nelson recalled the last time he saw Kathy in Austin, only a week before her death. "She had just turned twenty-three, but she had really grown much older. She looked too serious. She was worried about everything—money, making a living, was Charlie going to graduate or what. I think she would have divorced him eventually. I really do."

For fifty years, news reports on television and magazines have come and gone, marking morbid anniversary milestones since that terrible day in 1966. The temporary surges in public conversation remain painful for people who knew Kathy. Nelson has continued to visit his sister's grave privately, even when the popular narrative all but erased her.

"I'm sixty-nine years old now," Nelson said. "I often wonder what would have happened if she had married Lawrence. Had she, had she, had she . . . But that's not the way life is. It's kind of hard to release."

There is no negative for the original print at Adam's house, and Kathy's face will continue to fade.

But in this story, I discovered two images never captured on film, two images that will endure: In a driveway somewhere, the brother reaching down to lift a cardboard box of his sister's letters in his arms. The young girl years earlier scraping soil from her party shoes onto wax paper, as if to tell herself, as if to remind us all: I walked here. This earth is good.

Kathy with her little brother, Adam, not long before she was killed.

Photo Album

Kathy Leissner, 3 years old, in a portrait that appeared in a newspaper advertisement for Walker Studios: "Don't Take Chances on Something as Precious as Your Baby's Pictures"

Kathy and a friend on the first day of school

Kathy's 9th grade portrait

A more casual picture of Kathy during high school, in her parents' home

Senior year at Needville High School, 1961: Kathy (center) clowning with two friends and fellow volleyball players after losing the district championship. As art editor for the yearbook, Kathy made sure this photo made the cut.

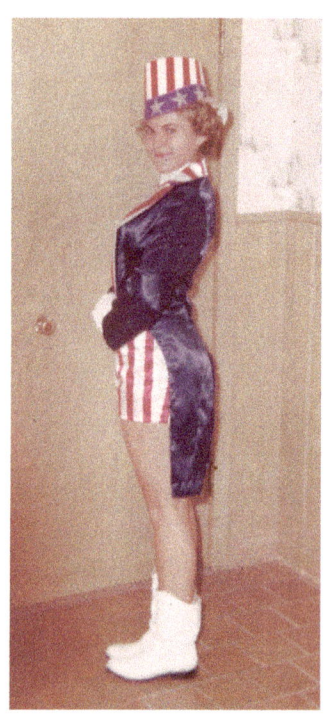

Kathy wore an Uncle Sam costume for a patriotic float in a local parade.

Charles Whitman in uniform, January 1962

Kathy at her bridal shower, July 1962

*Wedding day, 17 August 1962:
Kathy enters St. Michael's Church on the arm of
her father, Raymond Leissner.*

Newlyweds Kathy and Charlie Whitman share a kiss on the way to the car after the wedding reception held at her parents' home. Charlie's father, C. A. Whitman, in the background.

Nelson (center right) on a glass-bottom boat ride during his time with the Whitman family, August 1962.

From left to right: Charlie's brothers, Patrick and Johnnie Mike; his mother, Margaret; Nelson Leissner; Charlie's father, C.A. Whitman.

Johnny Mike was shot and killed during an argument at a bar in 1973; Patrick contracted AIDS and died in 1989.

Formal portrait of Kathy to Charlie (c. 1965), signed, "Yours until the end of always."

Kathy and Charlie outside her parents' home on a visit during military leave, 12 October 1963.

An uncomfortable photo on a serious day, 26 November 1963: Kathy joined her in-laws (C.A, far left, and Margaret) for Charlie's court martial at Camp Lejeune.

Note C.A.'s fingers and hand in the center of the image.

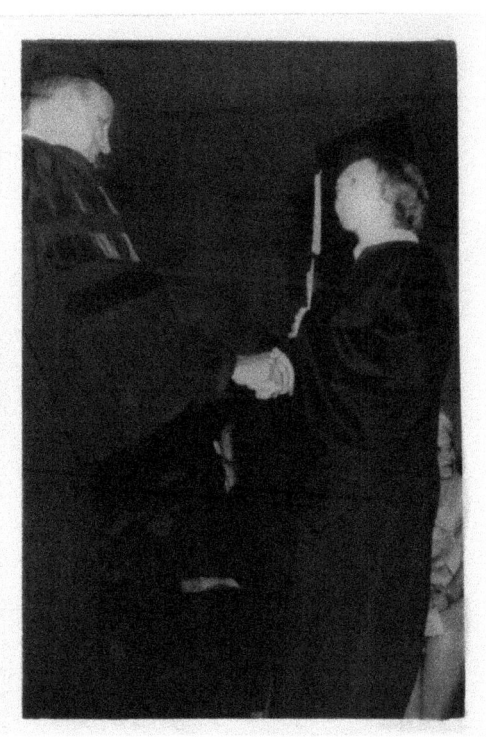

Kathy at graduation from UT Austin, 1965:
In a letter to her parents, she joked that this image showed her
receiving the piece of paper announcing how a diploma would arrive
by mail in six weeks.

*Nelson, with Adam on his shoulders,
during a visit to Barton Springs with Kathy and Charlie
a week before the murders*

*En route to her honeymoon, 17 August 1962:
Kathy Leissner waved farewell to family and friends.*

www.ingramcontent.com/pod-product-compliance
Lightning Source LLC
Chambersburg PA
CBHW062114290426
44110CB00023B/2806